My battles are your battles
Can't you see it?
Look into the mirror
I'm **you**
After a prison sentence.

The photographs on the inner covers show HMP Holloway, the women's
prison in North London to which Lady Unchained was sent aged 21.
HMP Holloway is set to be demolished this year (2022).
Picture credit: John Donat / RIBA Collections

brazen

Behind Bars

Lady Unchained

brazen

July 2022

First published in Great Britain in 2022 by Brazen,
an imprint of
Octopus Publishing Group Ltd
Carmelite House
50 Victoria Embankment
London EC4Y 0DZ
www.octopusbooks.co.uk

An Hachette UK Company
www.hachette.co.uk

Distributed in the US by
Hachette Book Group
1290 Avenue of the Americas
4th and 5th Floors
New York, NY 10104

Distributed in Canada by
Canadian Manda Group
664 Annette St.
Toronto, Ontario, Canada M6S 2C8

ISBN 978-1-91424-031-7

A CIP catalogue record for this book is available from the British Library.

Printed and bound in the UK

10 9 8 7 6 5 4 3 2 1

This FSC® label means that materials used for the product have been
responsibly sourced.

Dear **justice** system,
stop failing my **people**.

A voice for the voiceless

Contents

Unchained

My **nationality** does not define me
Yes, I am Black, African Black
And I guess that's all you see, but I am so much more.
I am Lady Unchained
I am **Unchained.**
I defeated the infection that we have grown to call a prison sentence
Which left untreated, can cause your mind to fall apart.
Haunted by the person you used to be, the person you used to know.
Why won't they just let me be me, why won't they just let me be free?
I wasn't born with the hunger to be free; I was born **free.** Nelson Mandela.
If he could sit down in a prison cell for decades, then who am to sit down and
    be defeated by this infectious curse that was created for us to believe that
    the truth is the lie, and the **lie** is the **truth**?
They used to **hang** us up in **trees** for everyone to see.
Lock us in **chains** to keep us in check.
Now they cast judgement in so-called courts of law and slander our names.
I mean why would our younger generations see themselves as anything
    different when you teach them the views that you wish still existed?
Instead, teach this generation we existed before we were slaves
We wasn't just made to be used and thrown away.
Wake up brothers and sisters!
Don't you see, we're just reliving the history that we've been taught to believe
I am not strange because of the colour of my skin
I am not a criminal or someone you should fear.

Crime & Punishment

I was on bail for around eight months before I went to jail. A lot of people are put on remand – I was lucky. Being on remand means you spend the time before your hearing in prison before going to a magistrates' court. But time spent on remand is later taken off your sentence. You don't get that on bail. In those eight months, I was going back and forth to court before being sentenced to two and a half years in prison at Inner London Crown Court (near Elephant and Castle). The prison you're allocated to is normally the one closest to the court you're sentenced in. I was sent to HMP Holloway. It was the only prison for women in London, so it felt like everyone got sent there.

Road to Victory

I await sentencing, scared and confused, but there's no praying
If God loved me then I wouldn't be in this mess, that's all I'm saying.
You're a female with no previous, you'll get off. You've got this, so stop fretting,
    I hear my friends say.
Yet my solicitor's voice rings loud, *you're looking at three to five, there's no doubt*
So just make sure you pack a bag each time you take that stand.
And still, I just can't quite understand.
But the judge soon makes it clear: he screams *two and a half! Take her away!*
Take me where?
I scream too, but there's no sound.
The waterfalls from my eyes kiss my cheeks. Farewell to me trying to look
    hard.
The life I once knew
Was no more.
Shattered dreams of future plans taken in a flash
Dark shadows and angry voices in my head telling me this is the end.

This is the end
So, just end it.

I left a piece of me on that stand.
I felt her walk away as I began to walk down them steps.
I swear I never even looked back.
See, I had to free her from this life that we were about to take.
Because she was the me with the dreams and ambitions
She was the me who still had faith in the so-called justice system
She was the me who prayed
She was the 11-year-old me who sang in Sunday choir
She was the me who wrote songs for Sunday school
She was the me who still cared about life.
All she was gonna do now was hold me back, with her dreams of the life that
    she once had.
Dreams were a thing of the past
Because where I was going, dreams are for the weak.
Forget love
I need respect
Because I ain't trying to be no-one's chick.
My beautiful future – no more.

And so, I began my life behind bars, broken and defeated.
Days were long, nights were longer, weekend bang-ups a lifetime.
Pain and tears were only to be felt at night.

Eleven-year-old me, where are you, I need you, where are you?
She returned to me in the form of a prayer:
Not long now girl, just stay strong. Pray to God and I promise you a better day.

All of a sudden, it just made sense.

This is the journey that was written for me to take

So I can teach my fellow brothers and sisters that

It's not about **anger;** it's about peace.

It's not about **power;** it's about grace.

It's not about **hatred;** it's about love.

These are the lessons I learnt while in prison, so you don't have to go there
to learn the same lessons.

The choice is yours,

I choose to be Unchained.

Strange Fruit

You didn't plant me
You planted the fear of us never being more than
    just your **slaves**
Your **property**
Your **fruit.**
You cannot pick me up and take a bite of me
I am not yours.
No wonder my brothers and sisters are sitting in
    jail cells
Thinking that they are fighting back by chaining
    themselves up.
Feeding on your hunger whilst their families
    starve.
We pay for the mistakes you make
While you just hide behind uniforms and badges
    that we will never understand.
The law is built to protect **you.**
I mean why else would you cast us away each time
    we come close to **unmasking** your disguise?
You kill one of our own to remind us who's in
    control,
And like the slaves we are
We turn on each other to please our masters –
Our masters who couldn't care less if we were here
    tomorrow.

I am Unchained.

When you're on bail, you can be given conditions such as curfews, tags or restrictions on where you can go. When I was on bail, I was told I couldn't go into the area of the club where the fight had happened. When I appeared at the magistrates' court for my hearing, I was warned my case would be allocated to the Crown Court immediately (magistrates' courts can't send you to prison). My solicitor told me to pack a bag of things I might need in prison each time I came to court.

Bail

Being on bail feels like a slow **death.**
Your body is left in **limbo**
As you watch the **life** you knew fall apart.
The smile you had turns into a frown,
Love into **hate,**
Anger and **regret.**
Bail tells you you're a **failure.**
Future plans **crashed**
Like taking a test and getting an 'F'.
Your words and voice no longer have **meaning.**
The *you* before bail no longer **exists**
No one wants to hear your **truth.**
You sit in court and listen to others
While they speak about the person you claim
    to be.
Yet, no one wants to hear you say a thing –
Solicitors tell you to pack your bag
Because each hearing could be
Your last **breath** before you're put into the ground.

The last time you hear your name out loud.
Before you're given a **number**
That will become your new identity.
The **criminal.**
The convict.
Convicted for a crime no one lets you explain –
Your ghostly body just watches on
As the judge **slams** the gavel
To alert you to the start of your **death** sentence.
No more limbo.
This is your casket.
This is your **funeral.**
You can't see your family
But you can hear their cries,
Their **screams.**
Their last sigh becomes your last sound
And only you can hear your screams.
You are no longer in limbo.
No longer on bail.
You are **dead**.

A sweatbox is a van that takes you to and from prisons. It's a box. It's tiny. I don't think I'm tall, but now and again, I'd have to turn in the seats to give my legs a break. There are no seat belts, so you slide all over the place. You can see out of the tinted windows, but no one can see in. You can hear everything and everyone in the van.

I'm an old soul – I listened to Magic FM growing up – and I remember they had *Easy (Like Sunday Morning)* playing on the radio. I started singing along. We passed bars with people sitting outside. I was listening to these songs, thinking this is the last time I'm going to hear any music I know. The drive to North London was quite quick. Suddenly HMP Holloway was right there, and it hit me. I realised I used to walk past Holloway with my sisters and cousins all the time and I'd never even noticed it.

Sweatbox

A quick pat-down
And you're pointed to the sweatbox.
Climb up the stairs,
Turn right
And take your seat.
To watch your life as it falls apart.

Watch the 'normals' live their lives
As yours comes to an end.
Loved ones holding hands,
Pubs still pouring pints.
You see everything through glass,
Yet no one sees you,
No one even knows you're there.

Would they even care?

Would you have cared?

Sitting in the sweatbox makes you question if you ever cared.

Will you ever care again?

Are you even worth caring for?

The Loved.

The Missed.

Will anyone remember your name?

Or will you just die inside?

Be forgotten like those who made the journey before you.

Driven through streets that remind you of your childhood,

A time before sweatboxes,

A time before prison sentences,

When blue t-shirts and grey tracksuit bottoms were just clothes,

Not prison garms.

When you walked past these prison walls,

Not once thinking that one day you would live behind those same walls.

Would it have even made a difference if you'd known?

The sweatbox is your last chance to reflect alone,

No matter how long or short the journey to prison is,

All these thoughts are just the beginning of a battle you can never
    prepare for.

The battle of deep inner conflict

Starting with your identity

Slowly stripped away

As you reach your final destination.

Into the land of fake egos,

Fake smiles,

Hidden tears.

The land of the nameless,
The voiceless.

The sweatbox is the last time to dream without bars
Live your last moments through the strangers you see on the streets.
The 'normals' who will sleep in their own beds tonight
Wake up next to someone they love not a random stranger.
Who will live the life you wished you still had
Because once you step off that sweatbox
There are no more wigs,
No more home sweet home,
No more friends,
No more mum's chicken and rice,
No more 'I love you'.
Just screams that start off scary
Until they become your normal.

Unwritten Crime

I'm shipped away –
Off to the land of dreams,
Off to be free, free from all our troubles.
To the land where *white* people live,
Our prayers have finally been answered.
At least that's what the people we left behind would
    think.
The ones who would later only ever see me as the girl
    who spoke their language well for a **British** girl.
The people who would never know how it felt to wait
    for a giro you knew may never come.
The lucky parents whose kids never had to pick them
    up off the ground because they heard fireworks and
    thought they were bombs.
The ones who believed London was the land of dreams
I'm sure they believed money grew on trees
A little shake here and a little shake there and all your
    troubles could disappear.
The ones too blind to see that this is where dreams are
    trapped.
In prison cells,
Deportation centres and
Mental homes.
In tower blocks and postcode wars,
Knife crime and
Gun crime.
Here we are the murderers and the victims
Sacrificing each other for a piece of the dream.
The dream of freedom promised to our ancestors

Is now the same one taking the **lives** and **minds** of our
   children.
Because in this land, those dreams are only for the rich.
Rich and **white**.
White is right, and being born Black?
Well, that's just an unwritten crime.
After all, this is the land where white people live.

A Mother's Choice

I am born.

Not given a *choice* to be born, just born.

Shot out of my seed coat for my leaves to grow,

Placed on the Earth that's meant to hold all of
God's creatures.

Yet, not given the choice of which part of this
earth I will grow from baby to toddler, from
toddler to child.

My mum had other plans

This was not a part of the Earth she wanted her
children to grow.

She had lost too many of her seeds here and
decided she could not see another die.

This land didn't have enough water or food for her
flowers to blossom

Their leaves were beginning to brown and fall
back to the ground.

I Can't Show You My Scars

I'm not saying I'm innocent.
I did what I did and so did they.
I was innocent back then, but I can't say the same for them.
Yet, I'm the one sitting in the dock.

How do you explain to a jury of your peers and a judge with your life in
    their hands
That you've never had control of this life that they say you've been given?
So, being judged is nothing new.
Explaining never got me nowhere, so why start now?
To become another puppet trying to tell their story to the deaf without BSL.
Tell me how you explain to people that you've been branded with an invisible
    marker only you can see?
Left with screams only your abuser can hear
So they can relive the trauma you fight to erase each day.

I can't show you my scars.
But if I could they would paint a map
Of each mistake that they let happen to me.
Back then, when I was meant to be the innocent one
I never planned for this to happen.
But then again, I never planned to be born.
I just was.

I never had a choice back then
Back then when I was the innocent one.
But I'm not saying I'm innocent now
I did what I did and so did they.
Yet, I'm the one sitting in the dock.

Having to explain all the wrongs that I've done.

But never receiving an explanation for the wrongs that were done to **me.**

Facing life for crimes of a life

You wished you could rewrite.

The Three Ms

They may not have guns
But they still kill us.
In mental homes,
In prisons,
In our own communities.
Tackled to the ground before we can answer.
Guilty first until we can prove our innocence.
While they justify their use of force, we're left
    crying out for **justice.**

Our children are dying on the same streets **built
    on the pain of black people.**
Fathers and mothers locked up in chains because
    of their skin tone.
Family's lives left in turmoil
Women left with leaking breasts with no baby to
    feed
Kids crying, hungry for their mother's love

And still I see no changes.
Just more lives TAKEN, BROKEN and
    ERASED.
I. Can't. Breathe. Has become our national
    anthem.
But one still falls every day;
We're playing a game of dominos we will never
    win.

Serve and protect
But they only protect white people.
Rich and white,
Poor and white still have a chance . . .
Because in front of the judge at least they have the
right-coloured skin.

What chance do we have?
Even when suited and booted, we still can't
change the colour of our skin.
The colour of **danger.**
The colour of **poverty.**
The colour of **guilt.**
The colour they **fear** is the same colour that makes
us fear *them.*
Makes us bleach our skin.
Made us hate the texture of our hair so we hide it
under wigs.
Our culture has been erased through history.
They call it gentrified; we call it **whitewashed.**
Brainwashed.

But they can't remove the culture from our veins
Because this blood that pumps through these
veins has the **dreams** of Martin Luther King,
The **anger** of Malcom X
And the **rhythm** of Maya Angelou.

Awaken the three Ms inside you.
Tell them we know 'why the caged bird sings'
And that the song it sings is as beautiful as it sounds,

But it is not a happy song
It's a song of **pain,**
The song of **war.**
The cries of our ancestors,
Heard afresh through the cries of our children.

Behind Bars

I was 21 when I went to prison. I was terrified. I had no idea what to expect. It was my first offence. Little did I know I was about to spend my sentence in three different prisons across the country: HMP Holloway in London, HMP Morton Hall in Lincolnshire and HMP Downview in Surrey.

Sentencing

The judge found me guilty
This much I know.
I'm walked down to the cells out of the courtroom.
The cold hits me like a slap in the face.
My tears have frozen
My escort speaks but the sound is blurred.
I'm still trying to understand if this is real
If the judge made a mistake.
I see my escort open the cell door.
Finally, her words become clear:
You're here, I'm putting you on your own, okay
        love?
My tears melt – that's how I say thank you now.
I walk in.
My cell has bars not a metal door.
I can see others pass before they're placed behind
        the door
Where they can be heard but not seen.
I must be lucky.
I see my solicitor approach.
I hope she's here to tell me the judge made
        a mistake.

But her face tells a different story.

She hands me a piece of paper

A note with all the names, numbers and addresses
    of the people I would now have to write
    letters to.

No more £5 T-Mobile vouchers.

No more texting.

No more Facebook posts.

Holloway would be my new address.

No Place Like Home

I left my fully furnished one bedroom flat with the bag I was told to pack the
   night before.
I left my L-shaped sofa sitting on my carpet and my flat-screen TV hanging
   on the wall.
I left my smile,
My instant weave,
My dignity
And my identity at the prison reception.
I'm escorted through the prison with shower gel in plastic packets and a see-
   through plastic bag with my prison-issued clothing.
The air has a scent of sadness.
Fear is disguised by loudness.
The sound of keys and voices on the radio remind me I'm being watched.
I've lost count of how many gates slam behind me.
Before I finally arrive in the induction wing.
This is the first time I see carpet again outside of my home
I feel a false sense of calm before I'm escorted to my dorm.
Two women are already inside
We greet each other without words.
Just eye contact confirming each other's existence.

I zoned out.
Only returning to my sad reality at the sound of the door slamming behind
   me.
I take a seat at the next available single bed by the ventilated window.
I remember my double bed covered in my teddy bears I set in their perfect
   place every morning,
The sound of dogs barking
And birds singing outside my window.

In here the only singing is the song of hidden cries.
I cornrowed my hair like I promised my family and friends I would
Before I knew my weave would be kidnapped on entry to this establishment.

The place where dreams come to die
And dying seems like an even better escape.
There's no place like home.
And this is no home.

The Women

I look at these women
young
old
grandmothers
mothers
daughters
children
Black
white
Asian
educated
uneducated
labelled
numbered
tainted
tortured.
They all look like me.
I see the same sad look in their eyes.
Powerless.
Less than those we left outside.
Learning to live behind a fake smile is the first
    thing we teach each other
as we watch the sun rise and set through bars.
Watch the world change around us through a
    screen.
We are the women who see too much
Who hear cries at night
but no one hears or sees us.

When I first went to prison, I told my family not to visit me anymore. I didn't see myself finishing my sentence alive. I didn't see the point in carrying on – I knew that when I got out all my work and studying would mean nothing because I'd have a criminal conviction. The irony was I'd looked at becoming a prison officer after college.

Keys to Freedom

It started with anger
Prayers that could have never saved me.
I blamed God for my pain –
See I put my life in his hands
But his hands must have been full
Because I slipped through the gaps and he
couldn't even lend a hand.
Instead, he sent me to jail,
Even sent a priest in his place to remind me of his
so-called 'love'.
In this place where love doesn't exist,
Smiles are short-lived,
Laughter is followed by tears, and tears are a sign
of weakness.
I guess you must not have heard my cry, from the
pits of hell,
When I placed my hand on your book of life and
prayed for you to take my life.
So, I sent back his love
Because in here, it's a matter of life and death.
And death seems to be the only option.
I said **death** seems to be the only option.

Code red.
Code black.

I swear I never tried to end my life.
The letter they found was not my suicide note.
It was my safety net
My little glimpse of hope.

But I can see how it looked
Lying there cold on that ground
With a letter by my side, non-responsive to
    your help.

I kissed death on the lips
Prison was my time out
My journey back to faith.
It wasn't until that moment I realised
I wanted to live and I wanted to live to the fullest.

So, prison became my church
Prayers became my daily meal
And faith led me back to Christ.
Because in there,
It's a matter of life and death
And I chose life.
Because death is no longer an option.

No Black Heroes

Where are all the Black heroes?
Can Black people even be seen as heroes?

I went from the girl next door
To the girl in chains.
From the child you can trust
To the child who should be contained.

Would you have called me a hero if she had died
    that night?
If I just stood there and watched my sister die?
Watched and let her attackers have their way
With a howl as I watched them carry her lifeless
    body away?

Would you call me a hero because I fought my
    sister's killers?
Labelled me the **brave girl** who tried to save my
    sister's life?
The **poor girl** who watched her own flesh and
    blood take their last breath before her very
    eyes?
Would my story be more understood if I was a
    little white girl?
With white tears only other white people could
    relate too.
Because only they know what loss really feels like.
Only they know what it feels like to be scared.
But I am no white girl.

I am Black.
So, I wasn't labelled brave
Self-defence never came up
Black people can't be scared.

Yet, in that moment
I was scared.

Scared of losing a sister.

I should have been more afraid of ending up in
the so-called justice system.

For the first five or six days, I stayed where all the new prisoners stay: on the 'Induction Landing'. Each cell had a TV, sink and toilet. All the furniture was screwed to the ground. We had access to a bible, a kettle and a flask. But it didn't prepare me for real prison life – this place had carpet! Here, I was in a cell of four before moving to a cell of six on the main wing. Even though they gave me two sachets of shampoo on arrival, I didn't have the courage to shower for a while. I was scared ... I'd heard stories. When the London riots happened in 2011, I heard they added even more bunks to these already overcrowded cells.

Inside Holloway

We eat and shit in the same place we lay our heads.
Even dogs don't eat where they shit.
But inmates are no one's best friend
We're placed in kennels most dog owners would never let their pets spend
    a night.

It's been a week now
I still haven't used the loo.
I sit on the edge of my metal bed and watch woman after woman release
    their waste
Envying their no fucks given attitude.
While my waste just builds up inside my body
Turning into unbearable pain.

The scent of other women's trips to the toilet is becoming harder to ignore.
I feel dirty
Like I'm covered in everyone's shit.

But I am still afraid to use the shower.

The stories of dropping the soap still play loud in my head.

I trust no one here but myself

But I can't watch my own back.

Can't afford to get into another fight

Even if it's in self-defence.

That's how I ended up here.

Sharing a toilet with strangers when you didn't even use public toilets on the
outside.

Smelling other women's metallic periods in a place where hygiene isn't a
priority.

This must be the smell of guilt.

The place where fear grows until you no longer recognise who you are,

Who you were,

Who you will become seems too far away to dream.

Still entrapped in your pain and fears

Because here you are no one's best friend.

No one's child.

No one's sibling.

Here no one cares.

No Sign of Weakness

I sit in my cell reading letters from my family
Tears rolling down my cheeks uncontrollably.
Walking out those gates is the fantasy.
Reminiscing about life through photos stuck on
my wall
Hot water a distant memory
Running to the window just to get some 'fresh' air
Buss a joke and pretend you're okay
Showing pain is a sign of weakness so you have to
man up.

I wrote notes to myself in prison to avoid getting into trouble. I learned it was safer to write these things down than say them out loud, especially in HMP Morton Hall, where I already felt like they had it in for me. I didn't realise at the time, but these notes became bars of poetry.

Therapy

I write to avoid getting into more trouble.
(Time inside always dragged.)
I'm drowning in my thoughts that only remind
    me of home.
Home.

I can see it, but it's out of my reach
This ain't home.

No matter how hard I try to make it feel the same,
Pictures on my wall
Warming up my heart.

Prison routines varied between HMP Holloway, Morton Hall and Downview, but a normal weekday routine would look something like this: the cell door is unlocked at 7.30am or 8am, followed by breakfast. Work or education between 9am and 11.30am. Back to the landing at 11.30am. Lunch around 12.15pm. Locked in until 1.45pm. Work or education from 2pm to 4.30pm, followed by 10 to 15 minutes of socialisation before dinner. On weekdays, dinner is at about 5.30pm, earlier on weekends. Locked up until the next day by 6.45pm. On weekends, there's no education but people still go to work. If you want to exercise, you come out of your cell and line up with the others on your wing. You have to be accompanied to the exercise area by an officer.

New Normal

Exercise ladies!
Exercise ladies!
They call it exercise.
For days –
Maybe weeks –
I watched them through bars,
Walking around like hamsters.

They look so stupid.
I won't do that.
They won't make a fool of me,
Ever.
The ladies tried to make me join
Come get some fresh air, they said
I stood firm.

My word is all I have here.
I reply with a solid *no*.
No *maybe*.
No *later*.

I am not a mug.
I refuse to be institutionalised,
In this institute
That refuses to realise
I am human.
But humans are adaptable.
We adapt to our environment.
So here I am,
Smoking rolls ups
And walking around in a fucking circle.
Like the hamsters.
All the things I promised I would never do
I accept now.
I am an inmate.
This is my new normal.

Racism in prison feels legal. Inmates can't raise awareness on social media the same way you can outside. If something racially aggravated happens in jail, the only people that know about it are the officer and the inmate. Most of the time it's shut down. Even if an inmate tells other inmates about it, what can they do?

Racism is still an issue in prison because people don't have the same rights. Our letters are checked by prison officers, and they can be restricted or 'lost'. Officers can block visitor requests too. When I was moved to HMP Downview, I realised the prison officers at HMP Morton Hall had been withholding post from my solicitors.

Dear PO Nameless

Dear PO Nameless,

The name's Lady Unchained – I told you I would come for you.
All I did was ask you for a transfer,
And yes, I committed a crime, but I owned up to it.
Wish I could say the same for you.
Do you remember me?
You requested we have a meeting
But that wasn't a meeting now, was it?
More like an ambush from you and your hench female officer.
I guess that was your threat to me.
Do you remember me now?

You asked me my nationality,
I replied *British*.
I guess that was the wrong answer.

Because you repeated the question.
So I repeated my answer.
See, I don't stutter.

Must have been funny
'Cause you and your fellow officer had a little laugh
While I just sat there questioning your sanity.
Yet I'm the one who's meant to be the criminal.
Come on.
You must remember me now?
Or was there so many of us that you lost count?

You took away all my rights
and said the only thing you could do for me was send me back to where I
    come from.
Kampala, Uganda.
You said it so naturally like you was my father.
Well hello long-lost father!

Do you remember me?
I told you, see,
You ain't sending me nowhere
Unless it's London, Manchester, Liverpool or Birmingham.
'Cause I know I got family there I can stay with.
You wasn't satisfied though so you gave me a date;
Ninth of August 2009 was set to be my deportation day
(Three days before my birthday).
And I can't lie I began to feel the pain
And I wanted you to feel it too.
But I know how that ends.
I kick you where it hurts

And I end up feeling even more pain.
Still don't remember me?
I stood up to leave.
See I knew we wasn't going anywhere
But your guard dog was on cue
She stood over me to show me who's boss.
Have you ever laughed with fear?
I couldn't believe this was real.
I was a foreign national prisoner with officers who truly had it out for me.
I only saw this sort of stuff on TV.
Still don't remember me?

Dear PO Nameless,
I don't know what I done to you
That's got you going on this personal vendetta
But when I get out
I'm gonna find you
And I'm gonna light up the darkness with my **words**.
Still don't remember me?
You will.

When I was transferred from HMP Holloway to HMP Morton Hall, we weren't allowed breaks. It was a long drive to Lincolnshire (nearly 150 miles) and the only reason we stopped was to pick up more prisoners. I was transferred to HMP Morton Hall because they claimed I was here illegally from Uganda. They tried to deport me. I'd been in the UK since I was a kid. I started a hunger strike as a last resort for my case to be heard.

Silent Protest

I lost more than my British citizenship in this
    place they call a centre for foreign nationals.
I lost my right to be seen or heard.
I was nobody.
An illegal alien here.
My South London English is foreign.

My words only make me look more aggressive,
More angry,
More Foreign,
More Black.
I can feel myself falling deeper into their trap.
I'm transforming into the girl they labelled me to be.
Stamped a sign on my forehead I've been fighting
    with words to erase.

Now I've found another way to fight the enemy
Even though it may end up only hurting me.
My body will speak the words my mouth can't
    express.

No more food shall pass these lips.
These lips that won't stop causing me harm.
With no food there will be no more words.
My body will speak the words my mouth can't
    express
When it begins to feed on its own flesh.
When I become a ghostly version of the girl they
    labelled me to be
Maybe then they will start to see and hear me.
Before I completely fade away.

My work now means I visit prisons and hold workshops. On visiting HMP Cookham Wood, I was given a frappuccino that looked like it came from Starbucks. I couldn't believe it. This shock stayed with me, and on a visit to HMP Pentonville, I wanted to see if the inmates' food had changed. It hadn't – it was still carbs, beans and bread.

At HMP Morton Hall, where this poem is based, we weren't allowed to take food back to our cells – we were only allowed to eat in the dining rooms. Breakfast was a boiled egg and tinned tomatoes. Lunch might be a hot meal or a baguette sandwich. Dinner was bread or a baguette. There were no hot dinners at weekends.

Dear Mum

Dear Mum,
I'm sorry.
I know I promised to be good
And I swear I've been trying to hold it down
But see this place just ain't for me.
These officers are more racist than the guy who used to live down the road.
The white British inmates are complaining that they ain't got enough white
     products on the canteen.
I personally wouldn't care if they did put jollof on the menu.

I just wanna get out this hellhole that they tried to disguise as a centre.
Did you notice I said 'white British'?
I just realised that I was different
See this place is making me question every single part of my identity.
Mum, I swear they're trying to kill me.

Remember, I told you on the weekends we might as well starve?
See we get breakfast in the morning; well, that's what they call it . . .
It's one boiled egg, tinned tomatoes, five chips. If you drop one, you're pissed.
And we can't even take food back to our rooms . . .
Sorry I mean **cells** –
I'm still getting used to the word 'cell'.

I feel like I'm wasting away, mum.
I'm fighting to make it through, but freedom of speech just don't apply here.
I made a comment about the food, and how the portions could be better.
You'd never believe what the officer replied when he heard . . .
Don't act like when you're on the out you get more food than this.
As if to imply, that I must not eat anywhere but here.
I buss a switch mum, I'm sorry.
But how can he just take the piss? Does my life not mean a thing?
Is my skin colour too dark for them to have respect for me?
Don't they see that I too having a beating heart just like them
And two eyes I use to see just how much **hatred** they have for me?
Hopefully my transfer comes through
So I can go back to normality.

Pray for me mum; because these people are moving mad
And I don't wanna get caught up in their web of lies and confusion.
You know me, I don't fight, that's the other me.
I don't know how she works; I can't control her.
But it's like they can see her anger through my eyes
Because I can feel her heat pumping through my chest.
Mum, I'm not sure how long I can hold her in . . .
I just pray this transfer comes quick.

In prison, you can choose to work or study. You get paid a small amount, but for education it's slightly less. At HMP Holloway, I worked on reception. Roles vary but generally each prison has jobs in the kitchen and laundry, the recycling area and managing prisoners' canteen requests. You could also work with healthcare staff or become a gym orderly, which I did for a bit. That role mostly involved cleaning up the gym, but I also got to learn how to be a fitness trainer. Other jobs were more factory-based, from making parts for aeroplanes to making inmates' uniforms. When I was at HMP Morton Hall, I was sewing clothes. It felt like slave labour.

The Letter B

I was meant to go to prison.
Not because I deserved it,
Not because I was a bad person,
But because God said so.

Foreign national prisoners don't need an education.
Going there is the end of your vacation.
So, forget about any connections you made through
    your life in the UK
Forget about future learning.
You're only a flight away from landing in a place you
    were taught to hate.

You'll learn to sew tracksuit bottoms and jackets that
    will be shipped out to all the British inmates

All the while wishing you were that piece of clothing
    free to travel back to where you belong.
So, you sew the letter B inside the leg of a tracksuit
    bottom hoping someone will question how it got
    there,
What it stood for,
Who marked this letter B in their tracksuit bottoms?
But no one ever writes.
No one ever asks.
That letter B was my message in a bottle.
From a place I thought I would never escape.
Until one day I was whisked away
After a hunger strike.
Suicide watch for me.
But no one watched the officers.
I was shipped away like those pieces of clothing that I
    wished I could one day become.

Back with British inmates
With British rights.
Allowed to have an education.
See **British** inmates *need* an education.
Going to prison is their chance to reflect and deal
    with any rejection they may have faced in the
    outside world.
Forced to rebuild any connections they may have lost,
Yet all the while no one questions whether these
    connections are negative or positive.
In Downview, I found the tracksuit bottoms with the
    letter B in them.
See, enhanced inmates get to do their own laundry.

So, I decided to keep a pair of tracksuit bottoms,
Turned them inside out
And there it was, the letter B
Sewed inside one of the legs.
I was my own message in a bottle.

This was my story to tell.
But it would be 12 years before I could tell it.

Because getting out of prison would be when my real
    sentence began.
I was meant to go to prison.
Not because I deserved it,
Not because I was a bad person,
but because God said so.

At HMP Morton Hall, there was no diversity among the staff. I remember there was only one Black prison officer, and he stood outside the gate. But it was different inside. Ethnic minorities were overrepresented. The handful of white British prisoners at HMP Morton Hall were there by request – it was closer to their families in Manchester. My family was hours away in London. Sorting visits was hard because my visitor requests were being blocked. The officers told me again and again that the visitor slots were fully booked. One day, a female prison officer stepped in. She must have known something wasn't right. She came to my cell and told me to give my requests directly to her. After that, they were automatically approved. When my family came to visit, I remember sitting in the visitor hall and looking at all the empty chairs around me. They didn't understand why I was so broken by the empty chairs.

My Land

I feel like my **mind's** been **hijacked**
Taken over by **dark** thoughts.
Inside I'm begging to be **heard**
Begging to be **seen.**

But all they see is my crime.
My **dark** skin.
My change of **tone.**
Fists rolled and **tears** running down my cheeks.
But **Black** tears don't count
– don't **hurt**
– don't *feel.*
I'm fighting a battle that can't be won

In this **body** that they told me was my **own.**

Lower your tone
Crack a **smile**
Act like you're not angry you was nearly deported
To a land you've only just learnt to call home.
Learnt to embrace.

Now I'm ANGRY.
You made me hate my **roots.**
My **culture**.
My care for all things **African** turned into **fear.**
Disgrace.
Disgust.
So, now I'm **pro-Black**.
It's the only way I can be.
Trying to make up for lost time
when I **denied** my **own**
Just to **fit** into a **land** that will never see me as its
    equal.

I'm that **one** that **made** it **out,**
Slipped through their fishing net.
Their net that only catches **Black** people
And enslaves them in **their way** of **life.**
Then **throws** them **back** to the **sea** when they
    believe they're no good to them.

It must **hurt** you that I finally **landed** on my feet
But I had to **drown** before I could **resurface**.
Had to **kill** the **slave** you **instilled** in me.

The British girl you sold a dream to
And understand that I was **UGANDAN** before
 I was **BRITISH.**
But I'm **SOUTH LONDON** through and
 through.
Girls from the **south** don't go down without
 a fight.
So, I dedicate this fight to you.
Dear **justice** system,
Stop failing my **people**.

Silent Choir

They sent me to jail to **break** my spirit
But I was broken before sentencing.

Each appearance in court stripping away a piece
    of my identity
Being judged by people who never knew me.

My life spread across sheets of white paper
That didn't tell my actual story.

Rehabilitation is what they said I need
Yet no one explained how this process worked.
I got sentenced to two and a half years in prison
But had to teach myself what 'rehabilitation' meant.

All the tears I cried alone behind those bars
Quickly disappeared through cracks I could never find.

Tears I never knew travelled to join a choir of
    women all scarred and broken like me.
The choir of silent songs sang in a language only we
    knew and only we heard.

Entry requirements are simple:
Have you been used and abused?
Do you have an addiction you use to cover up pain
Or, better yet, a partner who does?
It's like an advertisement for the best support centre
    in the UK

But none of those needs are addressed while at
 Her Majesty's pleasure.
So, we sing our painful song
In hope that one day we will be **seen**
Be **heard** for who we are not just our crimes.
Our mistakes.
The choir of broken women who sing loud at night
But no one hears their silent song.

Growing up, I'd always been more comfortable being around guys. The only time I'd really been around other girls was in secondary school. After the first couple of days and weeks in prison, I gradually saw the motherly versions of these women. They saw me as a young person in prison that needed looking out for. I saw a community and built a lot of relationships in prison that I haven't been able to form elsewhere, beyond close family.

Invisible Scars

Prison walls hide a woman's scars.
The scars we learn to hide on the outside with a
    smile
Or with makeup.
So no one talks about them.
The scars no one sees
Or hears.

Until they're forced to see them
Behind these prison walls.

We hide behind these scars
The ones nobody wants to see.
We call each other the same names the men we
    thought loved us called us
To make us feel **weak,**
Unlovable,
Unwanted.

Until a judge wants to know **more**
Your invisible scars are left wide open
To heal behind bars.

Where salt is slowly sprinkled into your open
    wounds
With other wounded mothers, daughters,
    grandmas and children.
All trying to find healing in this warzone of
    broken minds.
So, they call each other the names their abusers
    used to call them:
Weak women,
Unlovable women,
Unwanted women.

Until the judge wants to know more about the
    woman.
Her scars are left open to heal behind bars
Where salt is slowly sprinkled into her wound.

I feared kindness in prison. I didn't want people to know how broken I was, so I spoke my language: Luganda. But one of the inmates spoke this too and understood what I was saying. She pulled me aside and told me it was going to be OK. I found out she told people on the other landings to look out for me. It was nice, but I panicked. I didn't trust anyone yet, and I feared owing people favours. How was I going to 'repay' this debt? But she didn't want anything. She just wanted to make sure I was OK.

Healing Water

My tears have become a healing water
A way to overcome my loneliness.
My rejection from the place I once called home
The land that abandoned my childlike dreams.

I doubt myself
My worth.
My image has become a blurred reflection of the
        girl I used to know.
Kindness only showing me the misery that lives
        inside me.

I have become hostile to parts of myself I used to
        love.
Denying myself the ability to be human.
So I use healing waters
To see the me I used to be.
The girl that believed in me.

When I was in prison, the nights and weekends were often understaffed. On the weekend, you were more than likely locked up all day unless you had a visitor. Unlike weekdays, there was only essential work and no education. It was so traumatising. They would unlock your cell in the morning and say, 'hot water and back behind your doors'. So, you'd fill up your flask and return to your cell. But other landings might be open or free, while you were on lockdown. They could come and talk through the gates, but when you're on lockdown you weren't going anywhere.

The Inner Child

Sometimes I think I'm going mad
Like this body I live in is borrowed.
Made up of someone else's anger and pain
And not enough joy.
The *tone* I speak in does not belong to me
She sounds too broken and that just isn't me.

I sometimes see a glimpse of her in my reflection
But her scars cut deep from within.
Leaving my heart with a burning sensation
Like it's bleeding
And nothing to soak up its blood.

How does she live with all these feelings?
Hack hack hacking away at her soul.
Eyes red with no weed.
Closed without sleep.
I'm hungry but she won't eat.

I try to force-feed her with love.
Until she feels that deep down her inner child
Still **sees** all she feels.

Dear Diary,
Please show her this note.
Tell her together we can be whole.
My love will help us heal our scars from within.

Dear Diary,
Please tell her to let love in.

I was sentenced to two and a half years and served eleven months behind bars. I was released on license on 27th December 2009. One of my conditions was to remain on tag for five months – approval for an electronic tag depends on good behaviour and it's only on offer if you're serving less than three years. My other licensing condition was to remain on curfew from around 7pm to 7am. I used to rush back to my flat make sure I was home in time. After what seemed like an eternity behind bars, I thought a curfew would be a walk in the park. But I became anxious about leaving the flat in case I wasn't back in time. In case probation officers called me and I wasn't there. I stayed inside for two weeks out of fear before probation officers told me to go outside because the monitor wasn't picking up my movements.

While I was on license, the world outside my flat made me scared of being sent back to prison. I remained on license until August 2011, when the London riots took place. I remember my probation officer telling me to go straight home. It was the day I officially came off license, meaning I would no longer have contact with the probation team. He said if I was seen on CCTV during the times of the riots in my area, I would more than likely become a suspect.

27th December 2009

I.

Mum ...

I'm coming home!

My scream from beyond the prison wall reaches every mother waiting at the
gate to see their daughter's face

and feel that long-awaited embrace.

I remember it like it was yesterday:

27th December 2009.

II.

After serving eleven months inside, I was finally being released from prison.

Free from those four walls that saw me break down and weep from the
weakness brought on by all the shame and sadness.

Could this *really* be the end of all my pain?

III.

Hidden tag,

Sprint from New Cross station

Jump into African uncle's cab

Try to explain why I need him to make like Road Runner with that great
escape from Wile E. Coyote.

BEEP BEEP.

No time to explain.

The clock strikes 7pm.

But I can still hear the chains?

The keys and slamming of doors?

Prison life is calling.

A0423AD

You never forget your prison number; it always stays with you.
Why can I hear the officers welcoming me back?
I have watched them welcome back women like me.
Now I understand how and why these women ended up back inside with me.

IIII.
Every red light feels like an extra month back inside
But just one day back there may be the death of me.
Will they be waiting for me outside my door to take my flesh back to hell?
7.15pm and we pull up to my block
My heart racing.
I can hear the monitor phone ringing before I even buzz myself in:
Hello Hello
I'm so sorry
I'm here

Like I never left
Never got out from those four walls.

A prison away from prison.
No more going outside.
Outside is too dangerous.
Outside means waiting again for another Release Day.

Life After Prison

When I first came home from prison, it felt surreal. I hadn't held keys in my hand for 11 months. I'd never needed to. I'd had such a strict routine in prison, and now it was gone. When I heard my neighbour's keys through the walls on that first night home, I was convinced it was one of the prison officers coming to unlock my cell.

First Night Home

I've waited for this day.
I've cried hoping for this day.
I've dreamt of this day.

But when my mum handed me keys
It felt so strange to me.
See, where I come from, only the screws have keys
They use them to torture us mentally.
They remind us of our non-existent power,
Our mistakes,
Our shame.

Daughter . . . go on, open the door.
But these keys give me no power.
They don't fit in my hands like they used to.

I enter my home like a stranger,
Take in my surroundings.
It all looks the same.
TV on the wall
L-shaped sofa in the same place
Just like I dreamt it in jail.

I should be happy
more excited
But I'm nervous
And I don't know why.
I hide it well behind my smile.
Prison taught me that much.

So they leave me alone.
Convinced I'm okay by my smile
(sometimes it even deceives me
and has me believing I'm okay too).
But these scars are deep
Invisible to the naked eye.

In prison my mind was free
Yet out here only my body feels free.
My mind feels like it's still in HMP.
Maybe sleeping in my own bed will set me free?
Erase the pain of the brick they called a pillow
The screams of women who shouldn't have been there,
The banging of doors,
The shutting up of lives.

I'm awakened by the sound of keys,
Footsteps.
I need to get up.
Get dressed.
Before the officer sees me naked again
And blames me for not being dressed and ready in
        time.
Then I realise

I am already home.
This is my bed.
No one is coming to unlock me.
I have the keys.
But still, I have no power.
I guess that's what prison took from me.

People and charities that come into prisons, such as Clean Break, offer hope of rehabilitation, but I don't believe that prisons rehabilitate people. That work is done by the individual and fellow inmates. And, even though I had a good probation officer, it still felt like I was thrown back with nothing when I left prison.

I'm Not Okay

I'm not okay.
I smile,
but I'm not okay.

I laugh,
but I'm not okay.

I work,
live,
speak,
but I'm not okay.

I'm in limbo
like I died and no one knows.
They haven't found me yet.
Inside I'm screaming,
knocking down walls,
But they still don't hear me or
see me.

Please find me,
I'm not okay.

I'm just learning to survive
until one day maybe I can learn
to be okay.

Dear Oppressor

Dear Oppressor,
I dedicate this poem to you and your team
for all the times you told me I would always come back to prison.

The ones who told me my cell will always be home.
To the lucky souls who've never had to spend a night in prison because they
    were never caught
but judged me for the time I spent inside.

To the employers that never gave me the chance to change my circumstances,
it's all good, baby.

Dear Oppressor,
You stole my smile, but you can never have my mind.
Memories of your oppression only make me fight harder for change.
Your hatred has opened my heart for others like me,
those still oppressed by your rage concealed by a cage of their own regret,
The bodies and mind still trapped.
My words will help guide them to find their way back home,
This is my promise to you,
Dear oppressor.

When I was in prison, I saw people who had been released come back. Recalls can be common, because there's very little preparation for the real world when you leave. And, if you don't understand your license conditions, it's very easy to break them. For some people, being in jail means having a community. Even for me, I struggled being out of prison. I didn't want to go back, but at the time, it often felt like the easier option. I remember being so broken that I asked a police officer to arrest me. Luckily, he didn't. I just didn't feel like I had a life here. When you leave prison, you're not returning to the life you had before. You're returning to a whole different life. And it's hard.

You After a Sentence

My battles are your battles
Can't you see it?
Look into the mirror
I'm **you**
After a prison sentence.

My pain is *your* pain
And you don't even know it.
I felt just like you before I was able to feel
    anything at all.

Sometimes you must feel before you learn.
See I ain't trying to be Jesus
I don't have that kind of power
(sometimes I wish I did).
I would switch your shoes with mine

So you can see how quickly things can change for
you too.

The mind you thought you knew
The heart you thought would always love
The mouth that never had a bad thing to say
Can suddenly change.
Can you see it?

I'm **you**
After your sentence.

Justice

You think you know me
But I don't think you do.
You call me a MAD girl.
I say I'm
Made
Amazingly
Different

You say I'm violent.
I ask, what is self-defence?

If you hit me, do I not bleed like you?
When you hurt my feelings, are my tears a different colour from yours?

What is the real difference between **me** and you?
Do I scare you?

Because no matter how hard you knock me down,
I end up back on my feet

Does my success scare you?
Does my strength make you fear the power I hold?
The lives I could save,
the stories I could give life to –
stories that **break** through the prisons you have built.

You think you know me?
Well, I've met you before
I've met many like you.

People who bring me down
Those who don't want to see me rise
Who do everything in their power to stop my voice from being heard.

Did you think you could stop us from speaking?
Tell the world what *you* really are.
An evil system that can **never** be fair
That would rather punish us than help us grow.

Justice created by my blood and tears.

Storytelling Anthem

I am still haunted in the night
By that year.
Pinch me.
Say it ain't so.
Tell me it was all a dream.
Damn.
I wished it was all a dream.
So now I write to help others like me
Come into the light
Stop walking in the dark.
There's so much more to see.
Your past will only make you stronger.

And if they talk
Let them.
If they hate
Love them.

See, some people are prisoners of their minds.
That's not your fault.
You've got to live your own life.
You've got so many lives to save.
Yes, I said save.
Not many make it to tell it.
And yet, here I stand
I've made it.
I'm Unchained from the pain.
Take a deep breath,

Inhale,
Exhale.
Now share your story.

This poem refers to the second time I was in front of a judge after coming off license for my first offence. I went to prison in 2009. Two years after that, I was back in court for a separate offence. Two years after that, I was back in front of a judge for yet another offence.

Freedom

You tell yourself freedom is just around the corner
And when the prison gates open, you start to believe it,

Feel it and **see** it in the family that hugs you.
But no one tells you how easy it is for you to end up back inside.

Hugs only take the pain away for a day.
No one tells you the change of your tone can take you back to the place that
    nearly killed you by killing all hope within you.
Leaving darkness and anger to become the source of all your decision making.
Fuck the feds,
Fuck the system,
Fuck it all.

Until you're back in front of a judge,

Anger growing with each word read out.
I can hear the girl I left behind screaming get me out
Feel tears burn my cheeks
I'm like a volcano waiting to erupt
The ground beneath me is beginning to shake
I stand before my oppressor.
The spirits of my ancestors stand beside me.

We **know** how this ends
Their **sins**
Their **beliefs**
Their **fear** for all things with colour.

What is a justice system with **no justice?**
Created by white people
With white laws.
Only passed in white rooms
Before white judges
In white wigs
Who pass judgement on white paper.
What say you?
GUILTY,
GUILTY,
GUILTY.

I was summoned because the courts said I owed them 59 hours of community service for an order they had given me five years prior. I knew it was an error, but I was still afraid I could end up back in prison. I wanted nothing more than to defend myself, but I remembered how that had got me in trouble at HMP Morton Hall. So, I prepared for the worst. It was the first time I had faced a panel of all-female judges. When they said I was free to go, I wondered: was this women looking out for women? But they told me they recognised all the work I'd done over the last five years and that they had never seen a transformation like mine.

The Win

So, I'm back in front of a judge again.
This is mad
I thought this was done.
They say I owe 59 hours of community service from five years ago?
It's been so long I'd forgotten how **petty** the justice system was
Feeding off those who can't even feed their own families.

So, they rob,
Steal and sometimes kill,
fighting to keep the clothes on their backs.

Yet they still ask us why we cry?
Why we die?
Why we can't seem to get it right?

I'm in front of three female judges without committing another crime
I've already done my time.

But this would be my third strike.
Once again, I'm left sitting awaiting my judgment.
Praying in silence for the judges to see me for the me I am today
Not who I was back then.

Once again, I am seen but not heard.
The performer in me just wants to speak out
The inmate in me tells me to keep my mouth shut
The writer in me starts to take note of the story she's about to bring to life.

But this hearing is to be different from the ones I had before.
The prosecution and defence were on the same side –
My side.
They agreed they'd made a mistake.
The three female judges tell me I'm free to go.
I stand but my legs refuse to take steps
I'm like a toddler learning to walk.
Learning to live and speak words for the first time again
Learning to be free without having to go back to jail
Learning that sometimes you can win when placed in front of a judge
But remembering our wins always start because of our loss.

I believe there is life after prison if the right support is given. There is light at the end of the tunnel. But it's hard. It's taken me ten years to be seen and heard for my creativity and not my crime. It shouldn't take that long but because of the stigma and discrimination around criminal convictions, people often shy away from being public about it.

Ain't I a Woman?

Ain't I a woman?
Does my strength confuse you?
I can see it hurts when you see me smile.
Does my smile make you fear me?
Because all you know is that I'm known to be
    violent?
You heard I use my smile to disguise my anger.
You heard it right.
See my inner child is crying out for help.
Like Joelle Taylor said, 'some boys cry with their
    fists'.
Yes, I am a woman
Fighting through men to be heard.
My small voice doesn't even begin to break
    through the cracks of hench arms and skin
    that can be mistaken for stone.
So, I'm forced to
shout out.
Fight harder than the mandem,
Until I'm seen like one of the mandem.
Walk, talk and stand like the mandem,

Do you see me now?
Five-foot-six and still standing taller than all the
    mandem,
Went to jail before most of my mandem,
 So I built the Unchained road to free what we
    thought we had lost.

Yes, I am a woman
Because only a woman can see the things that I've
    seen and still find a way to protect our men.
Hold them close to our chest until they feel loved
    again.
So answer me this:
Without the girldem, can there be any mandem?
I am a woman.

I record a show with National Prison Radio, and I've had people message me when they get out of prison saying they listened to it every Saturday. When I'm recording, I often think about how these inmates could be listening while on lockdown at the weekend. I want to be visible with my work. I want people to know there is life after prison.

A Thin Line Between Good and Bad

A good person can turn into a bad person in a matter of seconds
It ain't hard.
I thought I was good.
Did all the right things to stay that way.

I had a good life ahead of me
So why did I destroy it?
I had a beautiful future
So why let someone pull me down?
I knew I was better than that
And that it shouldn't be about power
It should be about love.
But all these things put together
Can turn a good person bad.

So, when you make a mistake,
Correct it.
Because you know you're better than that mistake.
Be strong
And remember you're the one thing they're not –
You're smart.
Don't forget about the past

Instead use it to build your future.
Live for tomorrow
Not for right now.
Dry your eyes little sister
The pain won't last forever.
Words can't scar you
You are stronger than that.
But if you scar someone because of your hurt and your pain
That scar will not only hurt that person
But also you and the people you love most.

So, make a choice.
Live for right now
Or live for **tomorrow.**

I just hope you can live with that choice.
As for me,
I am living for your tomorrow.

Death or a Prison Sentence

We're losing our younger generations to the streets
Where they're being trained to remain slaves to a future with
    only two options:
Death or a prison sentence.
It's the only fact the streets are honest about.
The streets don't always start with abuse.
In the beginning it's about love, friendships, money, girls, flashy things.
But not everything that glitters is gold,
And all those shiny things come with an unwritten price:
Death or a prison sentence.
Stories of kill or be killed;
It's **you** or them.
As if one of you will be better off in the end.
Yet, the only thing that's promised is:
Death or a prison sentence.

False promises with a pinch of love
Can never be worth your life.
Yes, dreams can come true
But only if you're alive to see them through.

So, next time you're told to take an enemy's life, a brother, a son, partner
    or friend
Look in the mirror
Because that journey begins and ends with **you.**
Death or a prison sentence doesn't need to be your truth.

Learn to love and believe in yourself,
And you'll soon come to realise

You were made for greater goals,
Greater dreams.

Find your mission on this land and you will see
You weren't put on this earth to destroy it.
You were created to bring forth change.
Love your fellow man.
Bring about new life
And teach them new ways of life.

Death or a prison sentence
Were only designed to blind you from your true reality
And hold you back from your kingdom –
Don't let the streets take your **crown**.

The Forgotten People

Please stop killing us.
I speak for the forgotten people.
The ones you would rather see buried, tortured rather than face us.
We are not your slaves, your prisoners, and we will **never** be your property,
Not again.

I guess that's why you throw us in cages
Paint hateful words on our streets and throw rocks and stones in the form of
　　police brutality,
And **still** we rise.

Our bodies have been abused so many times throughout history you hoped
　　we'd be extinct.
We cry out with destruction and abuse because that's what you taught us
The one who inflicts the most pain is the master so stop asking how we got
　　this way.

Maybe ask yourself why your ancestors put mine in boxes they knew we could
　　never fit in?
And after fighting you with every breath
Sometimes their last
They started to break their own bones just to please you.
Not because they were weak
But because you oppressed their soul and spirit,
Their bodies weakened and their flesh started to lose their will to live.

I'm not here to pass blame or justify why there's so much bloodshed in a
　　society we claim works,
I'm here to ask you to stand up for human rights.

I'm here to ask you to stand up and speak out instead of avoiding the problem.

The problem that we see and still do nothing about.

I'm here to ask you to understand that we are all connected through sight, sound and touch.

And every time we look up, we see the same sky.

We breathe the same air.

And when we bleed, we bleed the same colour.

So, if Black people no longer exist, tell me who or what will be next

And are you willing to find out?

Or will you help me build an Unchained world where love is 'love every colour'?

Rise my nations, rise.

I recently visited the now-closed HMP Holloway to film a documentary. When I was walking around the building, I realised the silence was scarier than the noise had been. Prison was always loud, especially during 'freeflow' when you were allowed to move freely within the jail (there were still officers around). It was during those freeflow moments I remember looking around and thinking that there are so many women in jail. They were all different ages too, from young people to grandmothers. It had never registered with me before how many women were behind bars.

Returning to Holloway

I walk back into this prison freely.
This building that once nearly killed me.
Made me forget my name,
My identity,
My worth.

This is the place that was meant to fix me
But only highlighted my issues and gave me no outlet to release them.
Instead, they were trapped inside with me
Eating away at my insides while I tried to disguise my hunger to seem strong.

I should feel different this time
But this place brings back pain I thought had healed and tears I thought were
    all cried out.
They return to the surface like they never left.
Have I not healed?

Some things have changed:
The walls feel smaller
Its foundation is weaker.
I walk through gates I once had to wait for an officer to unlock.
I have become a tour guide for others seeking to understand and find meaning
in' this nightmare women like me have had to live through.

I feel the spirits of those whose stories remain trapped in the cracks.
They speak to me through the strips of paint falling off the walls
The rusting of the metal beds.
They remind me my story is not the first and won't be the last
I feel them as I take each step forward through dead silence.
The cold air is like their last breath of life used to help me walk through these
halls for the last time
They are the light that shines within me.

I suddenly realise
I've never walked these halls alone.
I have always walked with these women
I was just too trapped, too broken to see.
Any of these women could be me
They could be you.
The Women of Holloway.
The Women hidden Behind Bars.
Never to be seen or heard.

I am the voice of the Forgotten Women.
Hear us now.

Epilogue

I Come From . . .

I come from a place where you're either Ride
    or Die
Or someone's Victim.
Where Evil lies behind the brightness of smiles
Where we hide behind a screwface so we don't
    show fear
Where nightmares are disguised as Dreams
And Dreams are a Privilege.

I come from a place where fighting is taught from
    a young age.
A place where being young doesn't last long
So we're forced to become men and women before
    we fully understand the responsibilities that
    follow.

I come from a place where love isn't love unless it's
    followed by pain.
Where black eyes and emotional abuse are how
    someone shows you they love you.
Where little girls are taught that a boy hitting
    them means he likes them.

I come from a place where up is down
And the sky only looks blue for those who have
    never seen darkness.
A place where darkness follows me every step of
    the way

And giving into darkness sometimes seems like
    the only way.

But I also come from a place where I taught
    myself to love myself through darkness,
To love every scar I see in my reflection
That paints a map to the woman you see today.

I come from a place where chains are meant to be
    broken.
I come from Fire.
I come from The Unchained Tribe.

Author's Acknowledgements

Though many years have passed since I served my prison sentence, it still lives with me. I relive it through my poetry and the amazing people I work with behind bars.

I would like to dedicate this book to my two amazing brothers, Muchaila and Derrick, who can only watch over me from Heaven now. They saw talent and power deep within me even before I had discovered it myself and they taught me to walk with my head held high. Today their words and memory live on through the confidence and love they fed me. I thank God for making sure our paths crossed.

Lastly, I want to thank my Queen, my creator, my mother, Mummy Star: Teddy. Thank you for passing on your strength and never-ending love. Now let them talk.

This **brazen** book was created by
Publishing Director: Romilly Morgan
Senior Editor: Alex Stetter
Editor: Sarah Kyle
Art Director: Jaz Bahra
Cover Designer: Tom Etherington
Copyeditor: Natasha Onwuemezi
Typesetter: Jeremy Tilston
Senior Production Controller: Allison Gonsalves
Sales: Kevin Hawkins & Dominic Smith
Publicity & Marketing: Hazel O'Brien & Charlotte Sanders
Legal: Imogen Plouviez, Sasha Duszynska Lewis & Nicola Thatcher